Sounds All Around Us

What Is Sound?

Charlotte Guillain

Heinemann Library
Chicago, Illinois

www.heinemannraintree.com
Visit our website to find out
more information about
Heinemann-Raintree books.

To order:

☎ Phone 888-454-2279

🖳 Visit www.heinemannraintree.com
  to browse our catalog and order online.

© 2009 Heinemann Library
an imprint of Capstone Global Library, LLC
Chicago, Illinois

Customer Service: 888-454-2279

Visit our website at www.heinemannraintree.com

Edited by Rebecca Rissman, Charlotte Guillain, and
Catherine Veitch
Designed by Joanna Hinton-Malivoire
Photo research by Tracy Cummins and Tracey Engel
Printed and bound by South China Printing Company Ltd

13 12 11 10 09
10 9 8 7 6 5 4 3 2 1

Library of Congress Cataloging-in-Publication Data
Guillain, Charlotte.
What is sound? / Charlotte Guillain.
p. cm. -- (Sounds around us)
Includes bibliographical references and index.
ISBN 978-1-4329-3199-5 (hc) -- ISBN 978-1-4329-3205-3 (pb)
1. Sounds--Juvenile literature. 2. Sound-waves--Juvenile
literature. I. Title.
QC225.5.G85 2008
534--dc22
                        2008051681

Acknowledgments
The author and publishers are grateful to the following for
permission to reproduce copyright material: age footstock
pp. **7** (©Juan Biosca), **11** (©Javier Larrea), **14** (©Demetrio
Carrasco/Agency Jon Arnold Images), **23b** (©Demetrio
Carrasco/Agency Jon Arnold Images); Alamy pp. **4 top left**
(©UpperCut Images), **8** (©David Sanger), **9** (©I4images-music-
1), **12** (©stock shots by itani), **13** (©stock shots by itani), **16**
(©Redferns Music Picture Library), **21** (©David Wall), **23a**
(©David Wall), **23c** (©stock shots by itani); Getty Images pp.
6 (©Brett Froomer), **17** (©STOCK4B), **18** (©Gen Nishino), **19**
(©Nordic Photos/Lena Johansson); iStockPhoto pp. **4 bottom
right** (©Peeter Viisimaa), **4 top right** (©Frank Leung);
Photolibrary pp. **5** (©Juniors Bildarchiv), **10** (©Image Source),
15 (©Banana Stock), **20** (©AFLO Royalty Free); Shutterstock **p
4 bottom left** (©devi).

Cover photograph of a road worker digging up tarmac
reproduced with permission of Alamy (©Tim Cuff). Back cover
photograph of a referee blowing a whistle reproduced with
permission of Getty Images (©Stock 4B).

The publishers would like to thank Nancy Harris and Adriana
Scalise for their assistance in the preparation of this book.

Every effort has been made to contact copyright holders of
any material reproduced in this book. Any omissions will
be rectified in subsequent printings if notice is given to
the publisher.

Contents

Sounds

There are many different sounds.

We hear different sounds around us
every day.

What Is Sound?

When we play a guitar we hear a sound.

When we play a guitar we make the strings shake.

When we play a drum we hear
a sound.

When we play a drum we make the drum shake.

When we shake something we make a sound.

When we shake or vibrate something
we make a sound.

Sound Waves

When something vibrates, it makes the air vibrate.

sound wave

When the air vibrates it is called a
sound wave.

sound wave

Sound waves move through the
air to our ears.

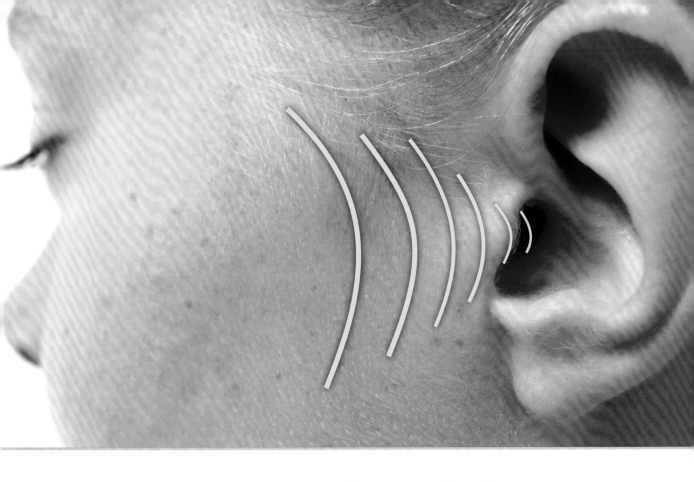

Sound waves move through the air
to our ears fast.

Our ears hear the sound.

Our ears hear the sound fast.

Sound waves can travel
through objects.

Sound waves can travel
through windows.

Echoes

Sound waves can repeat, or echo in buildings.

Sound waves can repeat, or echo in caves.

What Have You Learned?

- When something vibrates it makes a sound.

- When the air vibrates it is called a sound wave.

- We hear an echo when sound waves bounce back to us.

Picture Glossary

 **echo** when a sound comes back to you and you hear it again

 **sound wave** when the air shakes very quickly

 **vibrate** shake very quickly

Index

Note to Parents and Teachers
Before reading
Tell children that when something vibrates, it makes a sound. Hold up a musical triangle and play it. Have the children notice how the triangle vibrates when it is hit. Tell children that when the triangle vibrates it makes the air vibrate, and creates a sound wave. Tell children that when sound waves bounce back to us we hear an echo. Explain that an echo is when we hear the same sound again.

After reading
Try bouncing sound in this fun experiment. You will need one plate, several books, a ticking watch, a long cardboard tube, and two children. Build two piles of books that are the same height. Then lay the tube on the books. Ask child A to hold the watch to their ear. Instruct them to listen carefully to the ticking watch. Next ask child B to hold the watch at the far end of the tube. Tell child A to listen through the tube. Can they hear the watch? Ask child B to next hold a plate at the far end of the tube, behind the watch. Can child A hear the watch now? Discuss what has happened with the children. Explain that when the plate is put at the end of the tube, it makes the sound bounce back and forth creating an echo.